AGELESSYOU
ADVENTURE

LIVE AN EXTRAORDINARY LIFE

TOM FABBRI WITH
DR. ROXANNE CARFORA

ISBN: 0991172604
ISBN 13: 9780991172603

CONTENTS

CONTENTS

I dedicate this book to Rhonda Ann, for without her inspiration, belief, and undying love for me, this project would not have become a reality. She has shown me that anything is possible, and you can turn your life around, for the better, in an instant. I know this because she did it.

FOREWORD

At 22,600 feet, I look back to see Tom slowly falling behind the appropriately measured pace of the group. Descending back to him, I see he is obviously struggling. Every step is hard work, every breath labored and inadequate. Mount Aconcagua is extremely challenging, and we are close to the summit. Everyone struggles here. I talk with Tom, and together we push on. I watch as he digs deep through the discomfort, altitude, and cold, climbing the last couple of hundred feet to the summit. Standing on the highest point in South America at 22,837 feet, Tom and I hug. I can see in his eyes that he has accomplished one of his dreams.

A couple of years later, Tom and I are climbing again. This time we are working our way up the West Buttress of Denali, otherwise known as Mount McKinley, in Alaska. Around 16,700 feet, traversing the snow and rock ridge leading to high camp at 17,200 feet, Tom appears nervous. The ridge is difficult and exposed with thousands of feet of air on either side. At our next break, I ask about his tentative climbing.

He replies, "I'm afraid of heights."

Knowing Tom's determination, I respond, "Maybe consider a new passion." Although harsh, my comment is all it takes for him to sink his teeth in further. I know Tom won't give up. Climbing the last stretch to camp, he is extremely focused. When facing a challenge and confronting his fears, Tom thrives.

Tom Fabbri is an amazingly persistent and dedicated climber who works exceptionally hard to reach his goals. As a mountain guide, I have had the honor to work with Tom on two of his Seven Summits.

His ambition and motivation is inspiring, and I feel privileged to have shared these summits and dreams with him.

Geoff Schellens
RMI Mountain Guide
AMGA Certified Rock Guide

———

How the Good Life Is Killing Us

Whether it's climbing the Seven Summits, swimming with great whites, or becoming an airline captain, I understand firsthand the heights you can obtain once you give yourself permission to dream. I believe how we live our lives is not determined by how old we are or circumstances or the families we are born into. We have the ability to rise above any limitation, fear, or negative thoughts that keep us from finding the passion within us. We all have dreams. We've had them since our childhood, but somewhere along the way into adulthood, we lose the person we were born to be and become someone else's idea of who we should be.

Not only do we lose the dreams we once had, but our lifestyle in general over the last 50 years has slowly started killing us. In many ways it was a good thing "ease" and "comfort" became cultural norms after the Great Depression, which was just that—depressing. The world during that era included years of sacrifice, hardship, and tragedy. In those times preceding the 1950s, just getting through the day required real effort for most people.

Our world has changed since then, to say the very least. We have become more comfortable. Living, in many ways, has simply gotten easier, and we expect it to be easier and easier. The 1,250-square-foot dream house of our fathers—where they lived until they died—are now starter homes for young couples on their way to 3,000-square-foot mansions. Cars are cushier and come standard with air conditioning and other amenities, of course. The average hotel room is more luxurious, and work has turned from something you did, often with your hands, to someplace you go. When you get there, you sit in a chair (a really nice one) for most of the day until sooner rather later, you go home. Then, you and your family get back in the nice car with heated leather seats and go out to dinner. You come home, sit down on the couch, and watch television on a screen that costs half a month's salary (what your father spent on his first car). You retire for the night on a king-size bed in a master suite connected to a bathroom the size of the average kitchen in the 1940s.

Yes, things have definitely gotten better, but in many ways *we* have gotten much worse. Study after peer-reviewed study clearly shows that we are less happy, less fulfilled, and less healthy than we once were. At the same time, we are more stressed, more troubled, and more overweight than generations before us. For all of the improvements we have made in our lives, there seems to have been a cost—and it may have been us.

The way we have made our lives easier has made living altogether harder. It's harder on our bodies, harder on our minds, and harder on our overall happiness. Although modern medicine has us living longer, we seem to be getting older sooner than we should. The way we live, the food we eat, and the real work and effort we have designed out of our lives have all conspired against us. We have become what Dr. Brene Brown calls "the most in debt, obese, addicted, and medicated adult cohort in US history."

You don't have to be that way. You don't have to get older before you've gotten truly old. You can undo some of the ways in which you now live so you can truly enjoy the life you really deserve.

By making small, slow changes in how you spend your time, how you eat and drink and move, and even in how you think, you can become a different version of yourself. You can become ageless —

an "ageless" version of you. I know it is possible because I've done it. I am on a journey to climb the seven tallest peaks on the seven continents and then ski to the North and South Poles. This is what's called the Adventure Grand Slam, and only 40 people in the world have accomplished this, with only 11 of them being Americans. I have already successfully summited five of the seven peaks and will be embarking on the sixth one, Vinson Massif in Antarctica, in November 2015. I climbed four of these mountains in one year. I am 56 years old. Through each adventure, I have gained new experiences and insights about myself and what I am capable of. Completing the Adventure Grand Slam is my dream, but your dream could be anything you want it to be. The important thing is that you take the first step and go for it.

In this book, we will discuss the five areas of your life you can change to become healthier, more active, and more alive than you may have been in years. Success is the progression toward a worthy idea, and together we will formulate a plan for the changes you want to make, using real strategies that will turn those ideas into realities. Included in this book are tools for redefining your health and fitness goals, a discussion about the importance of your emotional well-being in living an effective and ageless life, and an exploration of healthy eating and exercise techniques I've developed—techniques that are truly sustainable and effective for anyone. Finally, I'll make sure you know how to have fun and adventure, not just with the positive changes you will make for yourself, but also with the rest of the extraordinary life you will live.

Some things are so much better than they used to be. It's time for you to make everything better. It's time for you to live the life you deserve. Your mountain, dream, passion, and purpose is waiting for you. It *is* possible, and it's not too late. I am very happy to offer this book, *Ageless You Adventure*. Come join me on an adventure into the completely better life you have earned for yourselves.

"We are all born with three things...a mind, a body, and a lifetime. How you use the first two determines the third."
—Anonymous

Tom Fabbri, 2014

———

CHAPTER 1

Adventure Life Now

Life Is an Adventure—Live Yours Now

"It is not the mountains we conquer, but ourselves."—Sir Edmund Hillary

You can live your own adventure life now. The only thing standing in your way is you. Adventure is not just for the young at heart. It is for anyone who can still dream or remember what it was like to have a dream. In an August 3, 2013, article featured in the *Huffington Post* titled "The Top 5 Regrets of the Dying," Joe Martino discusses the realizations of a palliative care nurse who worked with dying patients. The nurse recalls the number one regret among dying patients as this: "I wish I would have had the courage to live a life true to myself, not the life others expected of me." The nurse goes on to say, "when people realize their life is almost over and looks back on it, it's easy to see how many dreams have gone unfulfilled. Most people had to die knowing that it was due to choices they had made, or not made. Health brings freedom very few understand, until they no longer have it." In my opinion, it is very important to realize at least some of your dreams along the way because from the moment you lose your health, it's too late. I will show you the correlation between health and adventure throughout this book. You can't have one without the other.

Have you ever noticed how willing children are to be happy and adventurous? It's just one of the things we expect from them. When you see a four-year-old child running down the aisles of a supermarket and giggling out loud, you smile and think it's adorable. If you ever saw a 40 year-old man do the same thing, you would climb in with the frozen pizzas and call the police.

When we are young, real joy and happiness are natural parts of life. Fun and play are part of childhood, and for most of us, it is nurtured. Happiness—of the laughing and giggling variety—is encouraged when we are children; but for most of us, the lessons change as we get older. We start to hear things like "It's time to get serious," or "You can't do that," or the real bummer, "Stop acting like a kid!" So, many of us have learned to believe that real joy, adventure, and playtime are not necessary parts of adult life. Sure, we haven't given up on fun and adventure altogether, but we have made this one of our goals instead of an everyday (or at least a weekly) occurrence.

"Be happy for no reason, like a child. If you are happy for a reason, you're in trouble, because that reason can be taken from you."—Deepak Chopra

Why do we buy into that mindset? What is so wrong with acting like a kid sometimes? Children have a sense of wonder, of adventure, of play, and of happiness they long for and grab at every chance they get—these are truly the divine parts of being alive. We have somehow come to believe that shutting them down is a requirement of adult life, but this is one of the great tragedies in our culture—and it isn't true. Adventure and dreams and fun are the best parts of being an adult in the first place. What else is your health for but to share it with other people and to connect with the world around you? As you will see throughout this book, the purpose of making changes in your nutrition, exercise, and attitude is "to have more fun" in your life.

The interesting thing about happiness and health is that they feed off and need each other. The research on laughter and fun is clear: laughter is good for you, or actually, stress is bad for you; laughter, and joy, and playtime are powerful stress reducers. Laughter releases endorphins, which reduces stress and stress hormones. It lowers cortisol levels, creates a sense of well-being, and brings about peace. In terms of staying healthy and living longer, staying calm and free from the effects of chronic stress is vital. In a subsequent chapter of this book, I will show you the benefits of laughter to your health. Just as we need to seek out the right foods to eat, schedule time for our health, and take time to meditate and contemplate our goals, we must also take time for fun. We have to build some adventure into our lives.

For me, adventure is anything that pushes the limits of what I believe I am capable of. Climbing mountains happens to be the adventure of choice at this moment in my life. Chasing my dream of becoming the 12th American to climb the Seven Summits along with skiing to the North and South Poles is the ultimate challenge right now. Once I have successfully completed this endeavor, the sky is the limit for my next adventure, literally. I have my sights set on soaring into outer space…as a pilot, that is. After that, who knows? The point is to pursue your dreams, whatever they are, with passion and purpose.

Adventure and fun for you could be anything that motivates or challenges you in any way. They do not have to be made up of mythic quests and/or challenges. They do, like everything else you are doing for your health and emotional well-being, have to be a regular part of your life now. Adding adventure and fun to your life should be something you do on purpose and often. Taking time off for things that aren't work is essential to your health. It makes you even more productive and is the best part of the ageless lifestyle.

Discover Your Happiness—Again

In that same article from the *Huffington Post* on the top five regrets of the dying, the last regret was "I wish I had let myself be happier. Many did not realize that happiness is a choice, and so, they had stayed in old patterns and habits. The so-called 'comfort' of familiarity overflowed into their emotions as well as their physical lives. Fear of change had them pretending to others and to themselves that they were content, when deep inside they longed to laugh and have silliness in their lives again."

If you can't remember the last time you had real fun, it can be difficult to remember what fun actually is to you. I've seen it, and it's scary. If that's you, first spend some time reconnecting with your happiness. With nothing else on your mind, think about what makes you happy (or what used to make you happy) and write it down. Try to come up with at least five things that make you happier when you do them. I'm not going to offer suggestions—this one is on you. You may have forgotten, but if you think about it, you will remember who you are and what gives you joy. Try to remember five things and write them down.

Pause your reading and do this now.

Now that you have written down your five things (and this is the real genius part), do them. I know it sounds so obvious as to be stupid advice, but don't look at me—you're the one who hasn't done that thing you used to like so much. Seriously, right now have a look at your schedule for the next available open time slot that will allow you to do one of your five things, and put it on your schedule.

———

"Every moment in time is a moment in YOUR life.... LIVE IT!"

Adventure can make you happy, and you should always bring happiness on your adventures. When I go on adventures, I bring along what makes me happy—myself, my husband, my son, my daughter, my mother, my sister, my brother, or a friend. My list of five adventures is not as extreme as Tom's. He's extraordinary, and I am somewhat ordinary (only when it comes to *tall* mountains). I love to hike mini-mountains (maybe hills...ha, ha!) bike, walk on the beach, drive with my family to places we discover on the spur of the moment, and add a little "silly" to all of them. I have an adventure with my daughter every Sunday. We don't plan it. We just do it! We get in the car, turn on the radio, sing at the top our lungs, and just goooo! We always have fun no matter where our adventure brings us. Taking time to do things like this is so important. Cherish those moments, challenge yourself, and have *fun*! Sometimes not planning the adventure is the most memorable adventure of all....

Schedule Mini-Adventures

There is absolutely no need to wait until you have a long weekend or even some vacation time available to take a mini-vacation for a quick recharge. Consider scheduling simple three-hour adventures into your week. You can take your kids (or use that time to get a break from them), you can go with your significant other (or not), or you can even schedule some time with friends who you haven't connected with in a while—it doesn't matter. It is only important that you do it. Put the mini-vacation on your schedule. For example, "Thursday—6:00–9:00 p.m., meet friends for coffee" or "Wednesday—after work until whenever, take a walk in the park." Try once a week to schedule a little adventure away for the home and office for a quick recharge and time spent doing something else—anything else—anywhere. It doesn't matter.

If you don't like the park or coffee, do something else. Get a massage weekly. Go to the library or your favorite bookstore to read and meditate weekly. Making these activities part of your schedule makes them real. They deserve the same importance given to any other event on your calendar. You might decide Tuesday night is movie night—no matter what—and every Tuesday you are going to see a movie. (Note that horror movies are proven to be stressful, cortisol-increasing events that do not count as downtime.)

Have Fun Every Day

You can have adventure and fun at Starbucks. You can interact with the world by walking down the street where you live. You can play almost anywhere. The thing is, because we are adults, we have to do these things on purpose. Something, anything, should be fun for you every day. In my own life, I am very fortunate that I love cooking. The kitchen in my home is where I spend a lot of my day. There is something about the preparation of food, chopping vegetables, sautéing a piece of chicken, poaching eggs, and the wonderful smells that make cooking fun to me.

Every time I eat at home (or with a friend who lets me cook), I get 30 minutes to an hour of plain old fun before the meal. Now that I think about it, I even enjoy cleaning up after a meal.

If cooking is fun for you, then congratulations! You're there. If not, it is still important to do something every day that you enjoy doing. Make it a habit. If you like reading, do it every day. If you happen to love working out—and if you don't, be patient, it will come—then your workouts count as fun, too. A good friend of mine has a pool table in his garage and shoots for 30 minutes every day after work. If what really jazzes you is bird-watching, that's great! Now do it every day. If we're not careful, we will find ourselves looking back at this time (your life today) with longing for what we should have done more of—and it won't be the work. It will be the play, the connection, and the real time with those we love.

You don't have to have the same fun every day forever, but pick something daily and have fun with it on purpose. The reason is that if you can develop a habitual downtime rhythm to your life, your body and mind will start to know it is coming and act accordingly. What you are creating is a daily "light at the end of the tunnel." And yes, even if you are so fortunate to have a job you love to do and it energizes you, it still involves stresses on your brain and body. Having a daily period of something else that is not at all stressful becomes a very calming, steadying comfort in your life.

"A wasted weekend is not a weekend wasted."—Anonymous

Take Time Off—From Everything
The simple idea that "time doing nothing isn't actually doing nothing" isn't new and has never been bad advice. Your brain—like everything else—needs, or more correctly, grows, from downtime. You need time in your schedule when you consider absolutely nothing in particular. It is a lie to think that "achievement" is about

toil. It is a lie to think time off is laziness of any kind. Going to the beach or to the woods, spending time in the mountains or at a local park—even simply sitting in your backyard doing nothing at all but noticing the world around you—is a rejuvenating act of growth that will make your life and work better when you return.

In *Walden*, Henry David Thoreau put it this way—and I believe his thought is worth framing and putting on the wall in your office:

> *There were times when I could not afford to sacrifice the bloom of the present moment to any work, whether of the head or hands. I love a broad margin to my life. Sometimes, in a summer morning, having taken my accustomed bath, I sat in my sunny doorway from sunrise 'til noon, rapt in a revery, amidst the pines and hickories and sumachs, in undisturbed solitude and stillness, while the birds sang around or flitted noiseless through the house, until by the sun falling in at my west window, or the noise of some traveller's wagon on the distant highway, I was reminded of the lapse of time. I grew in those seasons like corn in the night, and they were far better than any work of the hands would have been. They were not time subtracted from my life, but so much over and above my usual allowance.*

In short, long hours of doing nothing is not *doing nothing*.

In conclusion, do you remember the goals you wrote down? Remember the purpose behind each one? I'm not sure if you noticed or not, but they all had to do with happiness, didn't they? The reason for every goal you have in life comes down to happiness and connection; and happiness is achieved when you stop waiting for it and make the most of the moment you're in now. The present moment is all about the fun and love and adventure of your life. You want more time with those you admire, more time laughing with your friends, and more time loving the person you are. Those are the only worthwhile reasons to be ageless.

You can reach those goals. You have everything you need to make the changes necessary to be healthier and happier. You can feel good about yourself every day. You can be more effective, have more energy and more vitality. You can forget your age and, quite literally, be ageless. Keep working, keep learning, and believe and start all of that right now. Begin living the way you deserve to live, and in no time, someone will ask, "How old are you?"

"I'm not" will be the truest answer you can give. Now go ahead: run down the aisle and laugh. Tell anyone who looks at you funny to lighten up—that's exactly what you did.

"ADVENTURE is the invitation to common people to become UNCOMMON."—Warren Miller

Calling home from the "roof of Africa", Mount Kilimanjaro

After battling rain, snow, fog and high winds, victory on the highest peak in Australia, Mt Kosciuszko

Promoting my 1st book "Ageless You" on the highest point in North America, Mt McKinley

Weathering a three day blizzard at 18,000 ft on Mt Aconcaqua

Tragedy on Aconcaqua – three members of this team perished in
the storm on the way to the summit

Waiting for good weather to fly off Kahiltna base camp on Mt McKinley

Celebrating after a successful summit on Mt. Aconcaqua with mule herders grilling Argentinian beef

The top of Russia, Mt Elbrus

Tragedy, a blizzard, and a lot of uncertainty made this summit,
Mt Aconcaqua, the most rewarding at 22,810ft

Selfie on Mt McKinley at 16,000 ft

Taking a well deserved break on Aconcaqua

Getting ready to break camp on Mt McKinley

———

CHAPTER 2

From Passion to Purpose

How I Became a World-Class Adventurer

**"PURPOSE is the reason for the journey.
PASSION is the fire that lights the way."**
—Anonymous

I n my quest to climb the Seven Summits, I have found a passion and purpose in my life I thought was part of my childhood… long past. As a kid, life is uninhibited. Somewhere, as we grow up, life ceases to be an adventure, and our dreams are set aside. When I am on top of a mountain, I am reminded of the importance of that moment and time in my life and how it makes me feel. I feel alive, empowered, inspired, and hopeful.

That moment of taking my passion and making it my purpose came at 40,000 feet in the air on a flight from Los Angeles to Cincinnati. I had an epiphany that I was supposed to be doing something bigger in my life. I was a captain at the airline and had achieved great success as a helicopter and jet pilot. I realized that if I could reach these heights after being told years earlier I was too old and not educated enough, then I could do anything I set my mind to do. I just had to believe in myself, set the goal, and take the necessary steps to move toward that goal. A great adventurer and friend of mine, Dick Rutan, put it best when he said, "If you can dream it, you can do it!" This became my path to become a world-class adventurer. I didn't begin this in my 20s, 30s, or even 40s. I started this journey in my 50s. Age, circumstance, background, or education should never stop you from pursuing your purpose in life.

There is nothing so common as our dreams for a better life. Almost everyone thinks about his or her future as different or better than now: "I'll make more money next year," "I'll be thinner next summer," "I'll be happier, more fulfilled, and have more fun in my life tomorrow." Hope is universal, but what isn't so common is hope fulfilled. Something seems to separate those who achieve their visions from those who only keep dreaming, or worse, lose that hope altogether.

That difference is purpose. Achievement of anything comes to those who take action—consistent and purposeful action—to reach their goals. This is true of finances and relationships. It's true of careers, and it is definitely true of health and fitness. Those who achieve their goals do more than just hope. They do something after they dream. They make plans and work their way into the futures they envision. By the end of this chapter, you will have defined your goals for agelessness and world- class health and laid the groundwork for the plan that will take you there.

———

"Sacrifices in life have a purpose.... Soon we recognize that PURPOSE becomes our PASSION."

W hat is your purpose, your passion? As a child, I always thought about becoming a doctor. I would watch *Marcus Welby, MD* (do you remember Dr. Marcus Welby? He is the title character in a medical drama series on ABC that aired from 1969 to 1976). This drama centered around a family practitioner and his assistant who were loved by their patients for their kind and caring bedside manners. I would run home from school and watch this show; it would later become my *life*. It became my purpose and journey to be the best doctor I could be. This did not come without a price, however. It was hard work: sleepless nights, missed family dinners, hours of study, and years of learning. Lots of sacrifice. (It's funny, the TV series did not show the sacrifices; they were hidden. Maybe it was because the end result was a happy doctor who enjoyed his profession and teaching others to do the same.) The sacrifices I have made served a purpose: to develop a passion to care for those in need, to fix those who are broken, and to do whatever I can to make their pain go away. It wasn't long before I realized this was my purpose in life. The hard work, the planning, the goal setting, the test taking, the failures and triumphs… it was all worth every second, every moment, every heartache!

Goal Setting and World Class Planning

"You are never too old to set another goal or to dream a new dream."—C. S. Lewis

Look at the difference between these two statements:

- I want to lose 20 pounds.
- By July 15, in order to be and feel healthier, I will lose 20 pounds through proper diet and consistent exercise.

They both say essentially the same thing—lose 20 pounds—but the second statement is much more powerful. It has a deadline and a purpose, and it just seems so much more achievable. That's because the first statement is raw hope, whereas the second is a goal with a plan.

To help goals become reality, four things should happen:

1. Make each goal specific, and give each goal a deadline.
2. Formulate a plan that makes sense.
3. Review the goal and its plan every day.
4. Remind yourself of the purpose and do the work.

These four steps turn goals into reality.

Step 1: Making Goals Specific

The most critical step in achieving success in any area of your life is to envision it as if it has already happened. Setting goals is the first step in turning the invisible into the visible. A clear picture of where you want to go is crucial to making it there. When I am on the mountain, I see myself on the summit before I have gotten there. It's not enough to say, "I hope I make it!" You need to have the added specifics that make the goal clear and achievable.

For each goal you have, you want to get to these specifics:

- Each goal should answer what, when, and why.
- Each goal should have a result, timeline, and purpose.

You can do this right now! Take out a blank sheet of paper and answer the following questions about your dreams:

"What" Questions

- **What are your dreams?** Be specific. Write them down no matter how big or small. Nothing is too detailed. For example, "I want to run a 10k" or "I want to climb Pikes Peak." These are specific, measurable things real goals start with.
- **What makes you happy?** Go back to your childhood and remember what you dreamed about as a child. Find the place that made you happy and fulfilled. As a child, we were not inhibited by what others thought. We were free to imagine being an astronaut, a ballerina, or a deep-sea adventurer.
- **What would it take to make your dreams real?** Figure out the steps you need to take financially, physically, and mentally to make your dreams happen. Don't get wrapped up in what you think your limits are. The how comes later. For now, just answer the questions as if you know it can be done. Visualize what you want and write it down.

Did you write down your answers? If not, stop just for a minute and consider taking this first step and putting down on paper what you want.

"When" Questions

Now we need to define the **when** for the **what** questions. It's been said that "a goal is a dream with a deadline." Sure, that's a little cliché, but there is a useful lesson for us here. You need to put a time line on your goals. You're going to use these answers to gauge your progress, adjust your plan, and create new goals when the time comes.

So next to each **what** answer, write down the answer about **when**. For instance, you want to climb a mountain. Great! By when? Here is where a good honest look at what you love is necessary. We live in the age of the "I can't" and "I'm too old." As I said in the beginning of this book, the ageless lifestyle isn't about limitations or impossibilities. It is about dreams.

How long did it take you to get to this place in your life in which you wanted to make a change, whether it's weight loss, a different career, finding happiness again, or living an unfulfilled dream? Well, chances are that it has taken a long time for you to get here, and changes won't happen overnight. The key, however, is to take the first step toward living the extraordinary life you were meant to live. You must decide now **what** you want to change and **when** you want to make the necessary changes (with specific dates—month, day, year). Post this information where you can see it.

"Why" Questions

You have asked the **what** and **when** questions. Now it's time to go back and think about **why** you want these things. This is one time where negative answers can actually help you. If your goal is to lose weight, your reason why may be, "I am tired of being overweight," but you can add a positive spin and say, "I want to feel and look my best." If you want to run a marathon, you might tell yourself that you are not a runner and could never do that; however, you could turn that around to say, "I may not be a runner, but I can do anything I set my mind to do." The negative can sometimes be as strong a motivator as the positive. Let yourself go deep into all the reasons you want the things you want. There are no wrong answers here. Be real with yourself. The key is not to lose sight of the goal and why you want it.

Having answered the **what**, **when**, and **why**, you now have written down a clear set of specific goals. You have taken your hopes and turned them into achievable ideas with a timeline for these achievements.

Step 2: Formulate a Plan for Success

The point is not to agonize over a specific day-to-day blueprint. You need to come up with actionable things to get you started. Let's be clear—the plan you start with now will not be the plan you finish with. You will adjust, change, and learn from the actions you take. Working a plan is about the small steps that will get you to your larger goal.

You may start with a plan to research what is involved in reaching your goal, such as training, financial obligation, and education. As you start to work your plan, you will get a better idea about its effectiveness. Your plan, like your goals, needs to be flexible—not to give yourself an "out" if you aren't reaching your goals, but to help you find ways to adjust your actions to help you meet your goals.

Yes, your deadlines might need to shift. You may reach them sooner than you thought, or perhaps you were too ambitious and need to change the plan. That's all fine. The important thing is to actually **have** a plan and work at it every day. The adjustments will come later.

As I stated before, success is the progression of a worthy ideal. **Your goals are the worthy ideal; the plan is a tool you will use to make the progression real.** Many of the questions you have about what to put into your plan and what to do first will be answered in the chapters that follow. When you come back to writing your initial plan, you will be able to use the information I have given you in this book to help formulate a plan. Your plan is something that needs to be written down. You can use journals or your computer, as long as you can easily and readily access the plan daily.

Step 3: Look at Your Goals Every Day
Looking at your goals every day is an important part of changing your behavior, and it is a behavioral shift that needs to take place to meet the deadlines you've set. Meeting deadlines require you to behave in a manner consistent with your goals. For that, you need to be reminded where you are heading every day. Otherwise, it is too easy to drift back to old habits. Keeping your goals "in your face," so to speak, makes it easier to act like you mean to achieve them.

If your goal is "I will lose 20 pounds in four weeks because the extra weight is affecting my heart," and you have that goal on your refrigerator, on your desk at work, or on a vision board in your bedroom, it becomes very hard to eat pizza for lunch. If eating pizza (or an equivalent "bad" food) for lunch was your old habit, seeing your goal in writing—along with the purpose for it—several times a day will help change that habit.

Seeing is believing. Physically seeing your deadline, goal, and reasons for the goal will make a believer out of you by influencing the decisions you make.

There are other things you can use to help you reach your goals that serve as constant daily reminders and help you make good decisions. Create a vision board with pictures of where you want to go, what you would like to look like, your dream house, the mountain you want to climb, the race you want to win…anything that will motivate you every day to move toward that goal.

Make copies of your goals. Read them every day. Put them in places that make it impossible for you not to see them. Adjust them as needed, cross them off when you reach them, and set them again, but keep them in front of you. Keep them on your mind, so the next step—actually doing the work—will be something you know you want to do.

Step 4: Doing the Work and Paying the Price

Paying the price...sounds dramatic, doesn't it? It isn't. If your dreams are big, and I hope they are, remember the steps to get there don't have to be. With your goals in front of you as constant daily reminders, following your plan and your visions will become realities by taking small manageable actions. A massive shift in your world doesn't have to occur.

You don't have to spend hours a day becoming a world class athlete, an Iron Chef, or an extreme adventurer. You don't have to completely change everything at once. Doing the work is about making small choices that will all add up and eventually bring you to the realization of those hopes you want to turn into goals.

Paying the price means giving up things that move you further from your goals. It may mean giving up a certain type of food for the sake of your health, getting up an hour earlier to fit something new into your schedule, or giving up your favorite television show for time used toward an activity that moves you closer to your goals.

Whether the timeline you set for your goals is measured in months or years, your goals will only come to you if you truly take action. Every day you will need to behave in a manner consistent with your goals.

"When you find your PURPOSE, you will find your PASSION."—Tom Fabbri

————

CHAPTER 3

Mind–Body–Soul Connection

The Importance of Unseen Things

"Every action and feeling is preceded by a thought."—James Allen

B e careful how you talk to yourself because you are listening. Many times what we think becomes reality. The first place we lose the battle is in our own thinking. If you think something is permanent, then it's permanent. If you think you've reached your limits, then you have. A great example of this was on my climb to the summit of Mount Aconcagua in Argentina. There were members of my team who had convinced themselves they would not reach the top. My tentmate was one of them. Ernest had confided in me that he believed he was the weakest man on the team and would not make it to the summit. On our way to high camp, we encountered a massive snowstorm with blizzard conditions that halted our ascent for three days. Nothing can play with your mind more than being stuck in a tent for three days waiting out a storm on the side of a mountain. Even I had doubts of getting to the top. During those days, I would journal about my fears, my dreams, my goals. I tried to encourage Ernest that he was stronger than he thought and could make it all the way. Ultimately nothing I said would make a difference; his mind was made up. He tried, but fell short of the summit.

We rarely want things for what they are. Instead we want things for how we think they will make us feel. If you want more money, it isn't because you like dollar bills; it's because you equate more money with less pressure, more fun, and an easier life. The feeling that "real" diamonds convey makes them more desirable than the equally brilliant cut glass. We all want the things we can see, but we desire the things we can't see.

If you want to be healthier, thinner, stronger, or anything else that can be seen, you have to consider (often) what unseen things you are really looking for. Our minds, bodies, and souls are not completely independent things. You cannot effectively change one without changing the others. If you want to improve your life and live an ageless, adventurous lifestyle, then you need to work on the unseen things in your life. You have to work on your mind, nurture your spirit, and feed your body, and then connect all of these to your life in meaningful ways.

Eat Like You Love Yourself
Move Like You Love Yourself
Speak Like You Love Yourself

The connection between what we want and why we want it is a positive and powerful thing, but it isn't enough just to brush by that truth and move on. We must pay attention to and nurture those things inside of us that make the outside world we want a reality.

Reading

"The man who doesn't read good books has no advantage over the man who can't read them."—Mark Twain

In our new, shiny digital world, it has become very easy to be a nonreader of what Twain called "good books." The web offers up a huge variety of things to read, but you have to be careful. Consider what you spend time reading—and almost as important, what you don't.

What you read is a diet for your mind just like food is for your body. Short reads like blog posts, magazine articles, and everything you ever read in the newspaper are snacks. They are always compressed versions of much larger ideas. Some of them are good snacks, and some are bad; either way, they are not enough. If you don't spend significant time reading, you are malnourishing your mind in the same way that snacking alone would malnourish your body.

Books (Twain's "good books") are deep and full explorations into broad ideas that truly inform your mind and intuition. They truly educate you in ways articles and blog posts cannot. Most important, taking in those complete and fully developed ideas allows you to credibly share that knowledge with those around you, just like properly nourishing your body allows you to do useful physical work.

Besides the deep exploration of full ideas that you get from them, reading books provides real downtime that web reading and TV (especially news shows) cannot. Sitting in your favorite chair, deeply engrossed in a good book with your thoughts, is deeply restorative. It is calming and just plain good for you.

In Tim Sanders's book *Love Is the Killer App* (read it), he espouses an 80/20 rule for books over articles (web or otherwise). Eighty percent of what you read should be books. Sanders calls them "thought meals"; articles, by comparison, are "ideas lite" or snacks. I couldn't agree more. Most of what you read should be the full, well-balanced meals provided in truly good books.

Fact or fiction: the 80% that Sanders speaks about shouldn't be made of modern fiction alone. You can spend a year reading nothing but Stephen King or J. K. Rowling, but it won't do much for you other than entertain your imagination. Fiction is fine, but you need balance in your book diet like you do in everything else. Read books on health and nutrition, for example. Learn things about relationships and communication. An excellent biography of someone you admire or respect is always great for motivation and inspiration and will help you to grow. Travel and adventure books will inspire you to dream.

In the end, you must grow your mind through reading and lifelong learning to really change the way you think, and therefore, how you act. If you take advantage of the benefits that reading provides, your physical and emotional transformation will be an easier and more lasting thing.

Journaling

"If your life's worth living, it's worth recording."—Tony Robbins

The next best practice to nurture the mind is to journal. Writing in a journal daily actually liberates the mind by giving the things you think about, worry about, dream about, and just mull over in your head every day a place to sit. The act of writing it all down allows you to let go of it long enough to work through those worries, fears, and thoughts and actually do something about them.

It's the same thing that happens when you make a list of any kind. For example, writing a simple grocery list allows you to literally forget about what you need and to carry those thoughts in your pocket. Imagine trying to carry that list of items in your head from your kitchen to the store. You always forget something that way. Journaling does to thoughts what lists do for the things you need: it allows you to let them go and to use your mind for the other things.

You should also write down what you are grateful for. Personally, I have found this to be a great stress reliever. By taking all of my thoughts and writing about them in my journal every morning, I reaffirm what I am grateful for in my life and what I need to work on to make things better. As I write about my goals and how I am progressing toward them, they are made more real for me and more present in my mind throughout the day.

You can do this electronically, but I prefer a really good quality notebook. By using something solid and well made, leather-covered with quality pages, it becomes a daily ritual and feels more permanent. When I start to feel that I'm not doing enough or my own progress is too slow, it helps to look back a few months (or years) and remind myself how far I have come. Journaling makes that possible in a way your memory cannot.

Thoughts Are Things

Another great habit to start doing is to say affirmations, or mantras. Yes, I mean saying things, positive things, out loud to yourself. So many of us have spent years playing tapes over and over in our heads that have talked us out of so much. Do you recognize any of these gems?

"I'll never have a home like that."
"She would never want to be with a guy like me."
"I'll never look like her."
"I can't reach the summit."
"Wow, it must be nice to…"

These things we say, both out loud and in our thoughts, have a profoundly negative effect on us. Whether we say them often or not, they are heard by our minds and always negatively affect our spirits. Remember my story about my tentmate, Ernest? Positive affirmations are a helpful way to undo the negativity those old phrases of lack and longing have wrought in our lives so far. You need to hear the words spoken out loud and in your ears. They will change how you feel about yourself, and how you feel about yourself determines the actions you take.

DR. ROXANNE CARFORA ON AFFIRMATIONS

As a physician, I have patients who say to me, "I can't do that," "I don't have the time," "I just don't have the desire," or "It's too expensive to be healthy." To those of you who may fit into one or more of these categories: "you can do it, you find the time, and the desire will then come." The strength is within each and every one of us, giving us the ability to achieve all goals. The best commitment you can make is to "self." In the course of my day, I always try to think of the positive. Recently, I attended a leukemia fundraiser for one of my patients who was getting ready for a bone transplant. His wife was raising money because the copays from the insurance company were so high. Jay is receiving chemotherapy on a daily basis and was so grateful for the celebration of his life. He was surrounded by friends and family. He is an artist and a fantastic painter. He has turned his cancer into a story. Jay said, "I WILL make this into a positive light in my life. I HAVE the desire to paint the images of what I am going through, and I HAVE time. I put NO PRICE on my health and will live my days being THANKFUL." As I walked around looking at the paintings and raffles, one painting stuck in my mind. Underneath it was one beautifully written sentence: **"YOU DON'T KNOW HOW STRONG YOU ARE UNTIL ALL YOU HAVE IS YOUR STRENGTH."** This strength is in all of us; it is part of our survival, and it is our beginning and end. Once we recognize it, we can push forward and make things happen.

How do your thoughts and words work to hold you back? What negative tapes have been playing over and over in your head? If you have been saying things like "It is so hard for me to lose weight," "I don't like going to the gym," or "I could never climb a mountain," then change the way you talk to yourself. Say things like "I am reaching my weight goals by eating healthy," "I love the feeling of accomplishment after I finish a workout," or "This mountain is not beyond my reach." It is often easier to say negative things to yourself. Get in the habit of saying the things you want for your life—out loud and often—and they will become easier to act on and to make real.

Release From Fear

"There are two basic motivating forces: fear and love. When we are afraid, we pull back from life. When we are in love, we are open to all that life has to offer with passion, excitement, and acceptance."—John Lennon

Fear is the single most destructive force in our human psyche when it's not used to our advantage. Will Smith describes it this way: "Fear is not real. It is a product of thoughts created. Do not misunderstand me; danger is very real, but fear is a choice." Most people let fear rule their lives. We are afraid of failure, ill health, criticism, death, and loss of love. Fear has two meanings: "Forget everything and run" or "Face everything and rise." We have a choice. Fear makes us want to take action—always—and when fear is unfounded, any action we take to ward off the danger can create unwanted consequences. For example, fear of rejection makes us keep people at arm's length so they can't reject us, right?

At the age of 28, I was cleaning and fueling helicopters and jets. The life of a pilot seemed very adventurous and exciting to me. I knew this was what I wanted to do with my life, but fear kept me in that comfortable place until one day I had the courage to ask one of the pilots what it would take to get in the pilot seat. His first question to me was "How old are you, Tom?" I told him, and he said I was probably too old. The next question was "Where did you go to college?" I told him that I didn't. He said to forget about it. That was the best advice he could have given me, because that rejection put a fire in me to prove him wrong. Not only did I become a pilot, I became a captain. That fear of rejection pushed me forward instead of holding me back.

Another fear I had to overcome was my fear of heights. "How can you have a fear of heights?" you might ask. I am a pilot, and I climb mountains—two activities where height is unavoidable. I choose to work through my fear and not let it stop me from doing what I want to do. It's a challenge I confront head-on. There is no greater feeling than flying 1,000 to 1,500 feet above New York City or reaching the summit of a mountain. The accomplishment of facing my fear and overcoming it is extremely gratifying.

Your Body Takes Notes

One of the most important factors in your overall health is how your mind can control your physical well-being. Studies have shown, most convincingly, that the fear of disease, even where there is not the slightest evidence of actual illness, often produces the physical symptoms of that disease.

In one analysis of 19 clinical trials of antidepressants that compared placebo control group results to actual users of the drugs, the expectation of the cure accounted for 75% of the drug's effectiveness—not related to chemical changes occurring in the brain. The quote "I think I am, therefore, I am" and the idea that a drug is effective because we believe it is can be instructive for us in our daily lives.

Dr. Paul Ekman, an expert on facial expressions and the author of numerous books on emotions, discovered that not only do our emotions play out on our faces, but if we mimic the expressions of emotion, we actually begin to feel physiological change because we made the faces. If you look up and smile, you become happier. If you make an angry facial expression, then you will begin to physically feel anger. The emotion and the outward evidence of the emotion are linked. In the same way, stress and anxiety (emotions that accompany real illness) have been linked to a higher incidence of illness. This is why it is so important to take care of your mind and emotional state as well. Stress and tension are real killers to your health. Happiness, being calm, and relaxation are truly good medicine. Your body listens to your mind for cues on how to feel. Tell it good things.

Discovering Your Soul
What we have discussed and will discuss in this book—from your goals and aspirations to the way you talk to yourself and take care of your body—are part of the discovery of who you truly are. All of this is about the outward manifestation of your authentic self. Like Michelangelo, who spoke of chipping away at the marble to remove everything that wasn't the figure inside, you also have to work on chipping away all of the things that aren't you.

The goals you set were about becoming what you want for yourself and how you see your own potential. They represent the you that is possible. To get to that person, you need to become that person emotionally as well. Your mind and spirit must match up with that better you first.

So, spend real time relaxing through meditation and reading. Write down your thoughts and dreams for the better life you envision. Talk to yourself and others about the real and positive things you want for your life. These unseen things are a real part of who you are, and their development shouldn't be left to circumstance. They deserve as much deliberate action as anything you will ever do in the gym or the office. How you nurture these unseen things is just as important as how you nurture your body. Your mind, body, and soul are connected, and changing one means changing the others.

"Being healthy is a way of life. It's not just about what you feed your body; it's about what you feed your mind and the social environment you keep."—Dr. Steve Maraboli

―――――

CHAPTER 4

Laughter Is Good Medicine

It's What Keeps You Young and Healthy

"Your sense of humor is one of the most powerful tools you have to make certain that your daily mood and emotional state supports good health."—Paul E. McGhee, PhD

Rx **Ageless You**
Dr. Roxanne Carfora

PRESCRIPTION TO A BETTER YOU

Laugh with a friend...
Its GREATER in Numbers!!

R. Carfora

uno/yous

G od has given us one of the greatest natural stress relievers known to man…LAUGHTER. Proverbs 17:22 says, "A happy heart is good medicine, and a cheerful mind works healing." I guess it's truthful to say, then, that laughter is like medicine, and best of all, this medicine is free, fun, and easy to use. It's medicine with no side effects, so please take regularly. Medical science tells us that laughing boosts our immune system. It reduces blood pressure and provides a good workout for our heart. Laughter, humor, and happiness also play a key role in positively affecting other diseases or conditions such as arthritis, diabetes, cancer, and many age-related chronic diseases that often cause disability. It can activate the body's natural tranquilizer to calm you and help you sleep better. Laughter is the antidote to stress, pain, and conflict.

Doctors are now recognizing the benefits of laughter as therapy for patients. Some pediatric hospitals are creating humor programs. An example of how well this kind of therapy works is a story I read of a 70 year old man with cancer. There was a shortage of beds in his hospital, and he was temporarily put on the pediatrics ward. He felt so much better after staying there that he asked to be with the kids the next time he was admitted. One in five national cancer institutes in the United States are now offering laughter and humor therapy.

DR. ROXANNE CARFORA ON LAUGHTER

I am a doctor, and I declare, **"Laughter is the BEST medicine you can give yourself and others."** Each and every one of us has a distinctive laugh. We are recognized by our laugh and are drawn to a room full of laughter. It is a positive response for all humans and is universal. There are no language barriers. We are born to laugh, and laughter takes very little energy to produce (although we all love to be tickled). Several years ago I took my staff to Puerto Rico for a weeklong vacation. Working every day can be very stressful, and I felt it was time for them to have a good time. I scheduled a sunrise yoga session that they were not too happy about. As the sun was rising, the yoga instructor told us to "take a deep breath in, slowly release it, and when we get to the last part of expiration…LAUGH IT OUT!" Well, we could not stop laughing. We were out of control, hysterically laughing! HAHAHA, HOHOHO, HEEEEHEEEE! We looked at one another and started laughing more and more, louder and louder. Our stomachs were hurting with so much laughter. It was the most we had laughed in such a long time! It turned out to be the best time of our lives! We still talk about it today. What a great way to celebrate with one another—through LAUGHTER!

Another hospital I read about takes long-term patients to the park a few hours a week to watch children playing. The original idea was to get them out of the hospital for relaxation, but the doctors discovered that watching the children laugh and play stimulated the patients' bodies' natural healing process. By just watching and hearing the children at play, the patients' outlooks changed, and they were able to recover more quickly. As you keep this in mind, know that the average child laughs more than 200 times a day, but the average adult laughs only 14 – 17 times a day.

Laughter provides a great distraction, as it takes the focus away from anger, guilt, stress, and negative emotions. Every time we laugh, we reduce the stress hormone and increase the production of the human growth hormone known as the "youth hormone." This can be as much as 87%. This hormone slows down the aging process and keeps you looking younger.

Laughter is contagious. It connects us with others and has the same effect as smiling and kindness. It can help you be more creative and solve problems. People who find time for humor and play in their daily lives find that it renews them and all of their relationships. As laughter, humor, and play become part of your life, your creativity will thrive, and opportunities to play with friends, coworkers, acquaintances, and loved ones will occur daily. Laughter can take you to a higher place where you view the world from a more relaxed, positive, creative, joyful, and balanced perspective.

Laughter makes you feel good, and this good feeling lasts even after the laughter subsides. Humor keeps you positive and optimistic through difficult situations, disappointments, and loss. It can give you courage, strength, and hope during difficult circumstances.

Create opportunities to laugh:

- Watch a funny movie or TV show.
- Go to a comedy club.

- Make time for fun activities.
- Play with your kids.

Laughter is a natural inborn part of life. Babies start smiling within the first weeks of life and laugh out loud within months of birth. Even if you did not grow up in a family where laughter was common, you can learn to laugh anytime. There are many ways to bring laughter and humor into your life. Here are a few ways to begin:

- **Smile:** Smiling is the beginning of laughter. It is as contagious as laughing.
- **Count your blessings:** Make a list of blessings in your life. Just the act of thinking about the good things in your life will steer you away from the negative thoughts, thereby creating an environment for laughter.
- **Spend time with fun, happy people:** These would be people who laugh easily at themselves and life's everyday events.
- **Laugh at situations rather than complain about them:** Look for the humor in a bad situation and see the irony life sometimes brings.
- **Surround yourself with reminders of something funny:** Reminders can be a funny poster, a computer screen saver that makes you laugh, or photos of you and your family having fun.
- **Keep things in perspective:** A lot of things in life are beyond our control, especially the behavior of other people.
- **Watch children and learn from them:** They are the experts on playing and laughing and being carefree.

We change physiologically when we laugh. We stretch muscles in and through our body and face. Some people say laughter can have similar benefits to those of a mild workout. The effects of laughter and exercise are very similar. Combining the two is a great way to boost your heart rate. William Fry, a pioneer in laughter research, claims it takes ten minutes on a rowing machine for his heart rate to reach the level it would after one minute of heavy laughter. Laughing appears to burn calories, too. Maciej Buchowski, a researcher from Vanderbilt University, did a small study in which he measured the amount of calories expended in laughing. He discovered that 10 -15 minutes of laughter burned 50 calories. This does not mean you need to stop your fitness program, but it is a fun way to burn a few extra calories.

A Laugh a Day Keeps the Doctor Away

According to recent studies by cardiologists at the University of Maryland Medical Center, this statement is truer than you think. Their study found that people with heart disease were 40% less likely to laugh compared to people of the same age without heart disease. "The old saying that 'laughter is the best medicine' definitely appears to be true when it comes to protecting your heart," says Michael Miller, MD, director of the Center for Preventive Cardiology at the University of Maryland Medical Center. "We don't know yet why laughing protects the heart, but we know that mental stress is associated with the impairment of the endothelium, the protective barrier lining our blood vessels. This can cause a series of inflammatory reactions that lead to fat and cholesterol buildup in the coronary arteries and ultimately to a heart attack."

In the course of this study, 300 participants, half of whom had heart disease, were given two questionnaires. One used a series of multiple-choice questions to find out how much or how little the participants laughed in certain situations. The second questionnaire used true or false choices to measure anger and hostility. Miller said that the most significant finding in the study was that "people with heart disease responded less humorously to everyday life situations, they laughed less, even in positive situations, and displayed more anger and hostility." Miller went on to say, "The recommendation for a healthy heart may one day be exercise, eating right, and laughing a few times a day."

"Always laugh when you can. It is cheap medicine."—Lord Byron

CHAPTER 5

Eating on Purpose

How to Feed Your Body the Right Way

"Diet has the distinction of being the only major determinate of health that is completely under your control. You have the final say over what does and does not go into your mouth and stomach. You cannot always control the other determinates of health, such as the quality of the air you breath, the noise you are subjected to, or the emotional climate of your surroundings, but you can control what you eat. It is a shame to squander such a good opportunity to influence your health."—Andrew Weil, MD, Natural Health, Natural Medicine

O f all the decisions we make in our lives, rarely is any as important as what we choose to eat and drink. When you first read this, it seems like an overstatement, I know. I'm not talking about what you ate last night, in particular. It's not about one meal or another, but rather what you choose to eat and drink consistently, most of the time. In this book, I share my experiences climbing mountains, but these adventures would not be possible if I didn't purposefully feed my body the proper nutrition it needs.

These decisions have a greater impact on your health and overall well-being than any others.

By comparison there are literally hundreds of exercise models out there: yoga, free weights, step aerobics, spin, Pilates, tai chi, running, etc., but which one you do is not nearly as important as the decision to work out in the first place. No exercise program makes things worse for you. That isn't true of food. The foods you eat matter a great deal. How you feed your body consistently will determine at least 80% of your success in achieving your health and fitness goals.

You've always known this. No adult has ever eaten a doughnut and thought, "This is exactly the kind of thing that will keep me slim." You know that what you eat matters—a lot—but to reach your goals, you are going to have to start consistently acting like you know it.

"Each meal is a new beginning...an opportunity to heal your body and change your life."—Katy S. Dougherty

———

"Food has a purpose! Eat lean and green, add some nuts and drink your water…. It's that simple."

We all know we are eating too many processed foods, too much cake, too much ice cream, too many hamburgers, too much bread, too much chocolate, too much of everything that is BAD for us. So why do we do it? How can we change our habits? How can we stay on track? We have to change our mind-set and realize everything we put in our body has a purpose, good and bad. Does that mean you can't have an occasional "treat"? No, but you may pay a price if you don't make the right choices. **Fruit has a purpose: an apple has 1,500 milligrams of vitamin C, 5 grams of fiber, and pectin for digestion. A chocolate doughnut serves no purpose: 50 grams of sugar, 1,000 grams of toxins, and acid for destruction, NOT digestion.** Fueling our bodies is the most important thing we can do every day. A car can't run on an empty tank, so why should we think our precious bodies can? Use the "rule of eights": eight hours of sleep, eight hours of work, eight hours of play. Be sure to fit in time to plan and prepare meals that will nourish your body, and **eat on purpose, for a purpose— LIVING.**

"Let food be thy medicine and medicine be thy food."— Hippocrates

Do you realize what this famous quote by Hippocrates, the father of modern medicine, is saying? Food heals…but not just any food, the right food. From the beginning of time, we have been given the perfect plan to nourish our bodies. Our ancestors ate from foods of the earth that included plants, seeds, fruits, vegetables, fowl from the air, fish from the sea, and animals that roamed and grazed the land. We changed the way food was intended for us to consume. In the process, we created a society facing the worst health crisis of our time or any other time. We have accepted disease as a normal part of life, and that does not have to be true. Our grandparents and great-grandparents of 100 years ago would not recognize the foods we eat today because 80% didn't exist then. Our foods have ingredients a mile long, with things in it that we can't even pronounce. Real food doesn't need an ingredient list because real food *IS* the ingredient.

We must rethink the way we think of food. Food is not something we consume just for pleasure; it is intended to nourish and heal our bodies. If we remind ourselves of the purpose of eating, we would make better choices.

"The food you eat can either be the safest and most powerful form of medicine or be the slowest form of poison."—Ann Wigmore

Small Steps
If you've developed eating habits that are, say, less than great, and the following nutritional advice represents a drastic change for you, then just like every other change, it will take time and patience to create. Drastic changes in diet rarely last. You can't go to the gym and exercise on the first day as if you had already been going for a

year. It takes time to adjust. Believe it or not, you will need to allow your body to adjust to new habits and new foods as well. The gradual move toward better eating habits will lead to a more permanent healthy lifestyle.

Listen to Your Body

This is one of the most important principles in this series of recommendations. If any food makes you sick in any way, stop consuming it immediately. Trust your body to provide you with better indications of what is good for you. When you follow this lifestyle plan, you will notice a remarkable improvement in the way you feel within a few days to a week; however, if anything makes you feel worse, remove it from your plan. I have laid out four steps to guide you in making the right choices and put you on a path to a healthier "ageless you."

Step 1: Avoid the Following Foods

The following foods are all highly allergenic and will frequently keep your immune system in overdrive by continually triggering the inflammatory response:

- **Wheat** (processed whole wheat products)
- **White Flour Products:** cookies, pastries, bread, baked goods
- **Pasteurized Milk and Dairy Products** (the pasteurization process kills any of the benefits of these products)
- **Highly Processed Grain-Based Products:** breads, pasta (multigrain can be eaten in moderation), cereal, bagels, French fries, chips, pretzels, frozen waffles and pancakes, packaged baked goods

For those of you who I just lost because you "love" bread or you can't live without French fries, don't despair just yet. Some very good alternatives

to those things you love so much do exist, and I promise you will find new
things to love as you slowly change the way you eat.

Step 2: Eat Live Foods

"What are 'live' foods?" you may be thinking. Foods that are plant-based in their original, uncooked state are considered raw and alive. Raw food includes fruits, vegetables, nuts, seeds, sprouts, grains, and fresh juices. These live foods contain a wide range of vital nutrients (vitamins, minerals, amino acids, oxygen) and live enzymes. Their nutritional properties are essential to the proper maintenance of human bodily functions. Many people eat plenty of calories and still suffer from malnutrition—nutrient deficiencies—by consuming a highly processed diet. As a result this leads to overeating and is one reason why many people cannot lose weight. If you consistently feel hungry, you're likely not getting sufficient amounts of the right nutrients your body needs to thrive.

At least one-third or more of our food should be uncooked. Valuable and sensitive micronutrients are damaged when we heat foods. Cooking and processing food can destroy these micronutrients by altering their shape and chemical composition. For our bodies to get benefits from cooked foods, our digestive system has to work longer and harder. This process can make our bodies feel heavy and tired. Raw foods are easy to digest and provide maximum amounts of energy with little effort. It makes sense, therefore, that live foods in their natural state can give us more energy and make us feel more alive. Studies have shown that live foods have healing powers that alleviate many illnesses, including cancer.

One of the best ways to incorporate raw, uncooked foods into our diet is juicing. This is the process of extracting juice from plant tissues such as those in fruits and vegetables. When you juice at home, you are assured of the freshest, healthiest, and best alternative to the juices you find in grocery stores. Most, or all, juices found in stores have been pasteurized, a heating technique that destroys the nutrients in raw plants. They are also loaded with sugar and other additives and very little real juice.

Juicing is not the only way to bring more live, uncooked foods into our ageless lifestyle, however. Salads made with spinach and other leafy greens, along with fresh fruits and vegetables; proteins such as chicken, turkey, or fish; and various nuts and seeds are a great way to get the benefits of the nutrients from these foods, as well as the fiber necessary to maintain a healthy functioning whole body. The addition of sprouts in our salad is another way to bring vital nutrients to a raw diet. Sprouts are living foods that are full of pure vitamins and minerals rich in chlorophyll and plant protein. The problem too many of us have with salads is what we choose to put on them—dressing. We have this idea that we are eating healthy by having the salad, but it turns unhealthy the minute we load it with heavy calorie-laden dressings. A simple dressing of olive oil and a splash of citrus such as orange, lemon, lime, or even some good balsamic vinegar is sufficient to make a salad healthy and pleasing for anyone.

I am not promoting any type of diet such as Paleo, vegetarian, or vegan. I am promoting eating for the whole body in a smart, purposeful way. As I stated earlier, about one-third of our diet should be uncooked. It is equally important that we prepare foods using the best oils, fats, salts, and seasonings that give our bodies the most benefits.

Step 3: All Sugars Are Not Created Equal

We eat more refined sugar today than our parents and grandparents did 30 or more years ago. As a result, obesity has risen to alarming rates in adults and children alike, and studies are finding more and more evidence that obesity is linked to cancer and other diseases.

Eating refined sugar weakens the immune system and promotes obesity, both of which are contributing factors to cancer. A weak immune system, in and of itself, is guaranteed to impair your health and promote virtually every disease known to humans. High sugar consumption can also lead to adrenal exhaustion and common symptoms that include mental and emotional stress, moodiness, salt and sugar cravings, and weakness and lethargy.

Every time you think about sugar—every time you read the word on an ingredient label—you should replace it with "cancer fuel" because that's what it is. It is cancer's "sweet tooth," if you will. Eliminating all sugar from your diet is not a good idea, however, as it would harm healthy cells that need energy to function. We have to understand there is a difference between natural sugar and refined or processed sugar. Our body's cells use sugar to keep our vital organs functioning; however, too much daily sugar causes weight gain—and unhealthy weight gain at that—along with a lack of exercise increase cancer risks. The daily recommendation of sugar is six tablespoons for women and nine tablespoons for men. Most Americans actually eat more than twice that amount of sugar in a day. This translates to about 500 calories that have no nutritional or cancer-fighting benefit. Processed sugar is not just limited to candy, pastries, or other foods we typically think of that are sweet. The problem is that within the processed sugar, "hidden" sugars are listed in its ingredients. Almost all processed foods on the market contain at least one of these sugars. Here is a list of some names to look out for:

- fructose (natural sugar from fruits)
- lactose (natural sugar from milk)
- sucrose (made from fructose and glucose)
- glucose (simple sugar, product of photosynthesis)
- dextrose (form of glucose)

Sugar is also disguised under the names of corn syrup, high-fructose corn syrup, maltodextrin, rice milk, white grape juice, brown rice syrup, date sugar, cane sugar, beet sugar, and sucanat.

Natural sugars such as fruits, molasses, raw honey, and unprocessed maple syrup are packed with antioxidants that protect our bodies from cancer. Keep in mind, however, that even though these are natural sugars, they must be consumed in moderation. The bottom line is sugar can fit into a healthy nutritional diet as long as it comes from organic fruits or other natural resources. Remember, it is always better to satisfy your sweet craving with nature and, at the same time, get more of the nutrients our bodies need to fight diseases like cancer, instead of feeding cancer with highly processed versions of sugar. Making smart food choices such as whole foods, lean protein, and complex carbohydrates will promote the long, healthy, ageless lifestyle we are all looking for.

Artificial sweeteners—all of them—should be avoided at all costs; they are simply toxic. More and more research states they could have devastating effects on our health. The consumption of diet sodas and other diet or low-fat products have increased dramatically over the last few years. Most people think that because a food has fewer calories or that it says "diet," they will lose weight. Actually, the opposite is true. Artificial sweeteners cause you to crave more sweet and sugary products.

Aspartame, the technical name for brands NutraSweet, Equal, Spoonful, and Equal-Measure, is "by far the most dangerous substance added to most foods today" according to Dr. Joseph Mercola. Researchers and physicians who study the adverse effects of aspartame believe the following chronic illnesses can be triggered or worsened by ingesting aspartame:

brain tumors
multiple sclerosis
epilepsy
Parkinson's disease
Alzheimer's
mental retardation

lymphoma
birth defects
fibromyalgia
diabetes

In the book *Prescription for Nutritional Healing* by James and Phyllis Balch, aspartame is listed under the category of "chemical poison" and with good reason. Aspartame is made up of three chemicals: aspartic acid (40%), phenylalanine (50%), and methanol (10%). In 1971 professor, neuroscientist, and researcher Dr. John Olney of Washington University School of Medicine informed the manufacturer of aspartame that aspartic acid caused holes in the brains of mice. Long-term use of phenylalanine has been known to cause schizophrenia and seizures, and methanol is a deadly poison. There are many products that should never have been approved for consumption, and this is one of them.

Step 4: Plan a Menu

Not "planning" to eat is a huge contributor to poor diet choice. If you don't plan ahead for lunch, ducking into the nearest restaurant is the easiest thing to do. If you don't think about what you will eat for dinner and make sure everything is ready, then ordering out is more likely to happen.

Most people have great difficulty implementing real nutritional change unless they sit down once a week (or a time when they are well rested, fresh, and relaxed) and plan every meal for the week ahead.

Yes, I suggest that you take a half hour to an hour out of your busy life and devote it to deciding what you are going to eat every week. I promise that doing so will not only make you healthier and give you more energy, but it will become one of your favorite things to do.

A great habit to start is preparing your meals ahead of time. For example, make your lunch for the next day before you go to bed. Decide what you will be eating for dinner before you leave the house in the morning. This allows you to go the store, if necessary, or take the appropriate items out of the freezer. The end of a tough day at work is not the time to test your willpower. However, if your dinner is planned and ready to go, the decision has been made, and you will eat in a manner consistent with your goals.

Not only is planning lunch and dinner important, but the one meal a lot of people will skimp on or skip all together is breakfast. It appears that our mothers were right when they told us that breakfast is the most important meal of the day. Studies show that eating a healthy breakfast (not the sugary cereal, frozen waffle, or doughnut kind) improves concentration, gives us more energy for physical activity, and even helps in weight control. Those who choose to start the day with a healthy meal will be less hungry during the day and will also make better food choices at other meals. You may think you are saving calories by skipping breakfast, but this is the wrong strategy. It actually causes you to eat more at lunch and throughout the day. A breakfast of protein, fruit, and a good whole grain such as steel-cut oats will give you the boost you need to keep you full until lunch. A traditional breakfast of eggs is the best way to get your morning protein. Despite being told that eggs are bad for us, they are considered one of the highest quality proteins.

Other Important Ingredients in a Healthy Nutritional Food Plan

Protein

Proteins are nutrients that are essential to the building, maintenance, and repair of our body tissues. They are also the major components of our immune system and hormones. Most people don't eat enough protein. A person's required protein intake varies and depends on your sex, height, weight, and exercise levels. Normal protein intake ranges from 20 grams to 50 grams at each meal. With that said, it is equally important to eat the right kind of protein. Acceptable proteins include organic eggs, grass-fed beef, free-range chicken or turkey, venison, and lamb. Fish is another excellent source of protein because it contains all the essential amino acids required for the body to grow and maintain lean muscle tissue. Amino acids are the building blocks that make up protein. There are nine essential amino acids the body cannot synthesize that must come through food protein. Vegetable protein is also acceptable, but should be combined with these other sources of lean proteins because vegetables do not contain any of the nine essential amino acids. Vegetable protein includes plants such as soybeans, spinach, green leaf lettuce, and fruits. Beans are a protein-rich superfood and are a great addition to any diet, especially for the vegetarian or vegan. Just half of a cup of beans contain as much protein as an ounce of steak, plus beans are loaded with fiber to keep you feeling full for hours. Some Greek yogurts contain high amounts of protein. As a rule when buying yogurt, however, you should buy plain yogurt and add your own sweetener (raw honey), fruits, nuts, raisins, dried cranberries, and sprinkle in some ground flaxseed.

Carbohydrates

Carbohydrates provide fuel for your body in the form of glucose or (good) sugar. (Remember, NO refined sugar.) There are two types of carbohydrates: simple and complex. Simple carbohydrates are sugars such as the ones found in candy, fruits, and baked goods. The simple sugar in fruit is the acceptable simple sugar; candy and baked goods contain refined sugar we have to avoid.

Complex carbohydrates are starches found in beans, nuts, vegetables, and whole grains. While both grains and vegetables are carbohydrates, most (not all) grains should be avoided, but most vegetables are acceptable. Your body prefers the carbohydrates in vegetables rather than grains because they slow the conversion to simple sugars like glucose and decreases your insulin level. Grain carbohydrates, on the other hand, will increase your insulin levels and interfere with your ability to burn fat. Acceptable carbohydrates are brown rice, steal-cut oats, rolled oats, quinoa, yams/sweet potatoes, and Ezekiel bread.

Fats

Fats can be confusing. Most people are convinced that too much fat in their diet makes them fat; however, the truth is that an extremely low-fat diet will not help you lose weight. In fact, if you don't get enough fat in your diet, you will be less healthy than if you are to include healthy fats in your meals. It is important to educate ourselves on the differences between "good" and "bad" fats. Omega-3 and omega-6 fats are some examples of good and bad fats. You may notice the phrase "good source of omega-3" on products at your local grocery store. This can be confusing if you do not know what omega-3 fats are. They are fatty acids found in the membranes of every cell in our bodies, and the only way we can get them is through the foods we eat. Omega-3 sources include eggs, flaxseed or flaxseed oil, pumpkin seeds, seafood, walnuts, and canola oil. Omega-6 fats, on the other hand, are considered bad fats if not eaten in moderation. We actually have way too much omega-6 fats in our diets compared to omega-3. Omega-6 acids promote inflammation, and omega-3 acids counter it. Examples of omega-6 are canola oil, corn oil, safflower oil, soybean oil, and sunflower oil. You will notice canola oil is on both lists. Although it is considered a healthier oil, there are twice as many omega-6 fats as there are omega-3, and it needs to be the opposite. It is important to keep this fact in mind when choosing cooking oil. The two best oils to use are olive oil and coconut oil.

When you go to the grocery store, you're confronted with advertisements telling you that a product is low in fat, or a product is made with partially hydrogenated oil. To make sense of all these labels, I've compiled the following list of definitions for you:

- **Saturated Fats:** These are found in animal products such as butter, cheese, whole milk, ice cream, and fatty meats. They are also found in some tropical plants and vegetables such as coconut, palm, and palm kernel. Some saturated fats are not as dangerous as you think. In fact, coconut is quite healthy and is one of the healthy oils I use for cooking because it is far less likely to be damaged through heating. A persistent fallacy is that saturated fat will increase your risk of heart attack. This is just another myth that has been harming your health for the last 30 or 40 years. The fact is that foods with saturated fats are nutritious and provide a concentrated source of energy in your diet. They are the building blocks for cell membrane and a variety of hormones and hormone- like substances. In addition, they act as carriers for important fat-soluble vitamins A, D, E, and K.
- **Trans Fats:** These fats form when vegetable oil hardens, a process called hydrogenation. These fats can raise LDL (bad cholesterol) levels and lower HDL (good cholesterol) levels, which of course is the complete **opposite** of what you need to maintain good heart health. In fact, trans fats—as opposed to saturated fats—have been linked to heart disease, clogging of the arteries, type 2 diabetes, and other serious health problems.
- **Monounsaturated Fats:** These are oils that are liquid at room temperature and semisolid when refrigerated. Extra virgin olive oil is the best example of a monounsaturated fat. Due to its high concentration of monounsaturated fat, olive oil can actually help to lower LDL (bad) cholesterol. This is the reason it is considered to be so healthy for

us. The Mediterranean diet, which is rich in olive oil, fruits, vegetables, and grains, helps to explain the lower rates of heart disease in countries such as Italy, Spain, and Greece, where people consume more than one-third of their daily calories from fats high in monounsaturated fatty acids. These fats help lower total cholesterol and LDL cholesterol. Simply put, olive oil is one of the best ways to add good fat to your diet and avoid bad fat.

What to Drink

By far the most important element of your diet is **water.**

Water makes up more than 70% of your body's tissues and plays a role in nearly every body function, from regulating temperature and cushioning joints to bringing oxygen to your cells and removing waste from your body.

Drinking enough water is one of the most simple, basic, and important health steps you can take. If you drink the required amount of water to maintain a light yellow coloring of your urine, you can easily avoid dehydration. This can have profound effects on your health. You can be dehydrated (or less than optimally hydrated) and not feel thirsty. Dehydration can also cause fatigue, dry skin, headaches, and constipation.

There has been a significant increase in the consumption of high-calorie drinks in recent years. From all the things we add to our coffee to the new energy drinks to sodas, some of us are consuming a day's worth of calories in a cup or can. These calories have no redeeming value. In fact, they are doing great harm. One piece of advice everyone should take is to **avoid ALL soft drinks.** Both regular and diet sodas are huge contributors to a number of health challenges. For example, did you know that for every can of soda you drink per day, your risk of obesity increases by 60 percent? Also, did you know it would take a four-mile run or 42 minute walk to burn off the calories in a 16 ounce bottle of soda? Eliminating soft drinks is one of the easiest changes you can make to significantly improve your health.

As far as fruit juices from the local grocery store are concerned, I personally don't drink them. As I have stated before, they contain only a small amount of real juice and are loaded with sugar and other additives. I prefer to make my own juice from whole fresh fruits and vegetables.

————

CHAPTER 6

Ten "Ageless" Recipes

"You don't have to cook fancy or complicated masterpieces—just good food from fresh ingredients."—Julia Child

C ooking skills used to be passed down from generation to generation, but this is not the case anymore. We now have generations who lack even the most basic skills. We must get back to the fundamentals of cooking because it is one of the easiest and best ways to control what goes onto our plates. What better way to assure that the right oils, the best salt, and the best ingredients with no unwanted additives are in our meals than to prepare them ourselves?.

Chicken Fiesta Soup with Beans and Rice

2 skinless chicken breasts, bone in
½ yellow onion, chopped
1 green pepper, chopped
1 red pepper, chopped
1 yellow pepper, chopped
1 orange pepper, chopped
½ cup cilantro, chopped
4 tomatoes, juiced
1 cup brown or basmati rice
1 box red kidney beans (Whole Foods 365 brand), drained and rinsed
2 boxes low-sodium vegetable stock (Whole Foods 365 brand)
Himalayan salt, to taste
Black pepper, to taste

Cook rice according to instructions on the package. Set aside. In a large stockpot, combine all ingredients, including rice, and bring to a boil on high heat. Reduce heat to medium to low and simmer for about 45 minutes. Remove the chicken from the soup, take off bone, and chop. Place back in pot and continue to cook for about 15 more minutes. This soup is great as a leftover the next day.

Stir-Fry Vegetables with Roasted Chicken

2 boneless, skinless chicken breasts, roasted
½ yellow squash, chopped
¼ yellow onion, chopped
1 ear of corn, kernels removed
4 broccoli florets
5 grape tomatoes, halved
2 tablespoons extra virgin olive oil
Himalayan salt, to taste
Black pepper, to taste

Preheat oven to 375 degrees. Heat olive oil in an ovenproof skillet on the stove on medium heat. Season chicken breasts with salt and pepper. Place chicken in skillet to sear on one side for about 2 minutes or until it pulls away from pan. Turn chicken on other side and place in the oven for about 10 minutes or until chicken is cooked through. Remove chicken from pan and cover to keep warm. Add the chopped vegetables, except the tomatoes, to the hot olive oil. Cook on medium heat. Add extra olive oil if needed. Stir the vegetables until tender, but not too done, adding salt and pepper, to taste. Be sure to use a potholder or kitchen towel around the handle of the pan as it will be very hot. Turn off heat and add tomatoes. Slice chicken breasts and place on top of vegetables. Serves two.

Key West Chicken Salad with Mango and Avocado

1 or 2 boneless, skinless chicken breasts, grilled or roasted
2 cups baby spinach
1 medium avocado, chopped
½ lime, squeezed
1 tablespoon cilantro, chopped
1 mango, chopped

Toss ingredients into a large bowl and enjoy.

Ratatouille Stew

1 small yellow onion, chopped
2 cloves of garlic, minced
3 medium tomatoes, peeled and quartered
1 green pepper, chopped
1 red pepper, chopped
1 yellow pepper, chopped
1 orange pepper, chopped
1 yellow squash, chopped
1 zucchini, chopped
2 red potatoes, chopped
2 purple potatoes, chopped (substitute more red potatoes if purple not available)
1 ear of corn, kernels removed
½ ground turkey or grass-fed ground beef, browned (optional)
2 tablespoons extra virgin olive oil
Himalayan salt, to taste
Black pepper, to taste

In a large Dutch oven or stockpot, sauté onions, garlic, and tomatoes in olive oil over medium heat. Be careful not to burn the garlic. Add the remaining ingredients except ground turkey, and season to taste. Cover with lid and simmer for 45 minutes on low heat. Brown ground turkey and add to stew, if so desired. Cook an additional 15 minutes to let the flavors of the vegetables cook with the meat.

Green Smoothie

1 ripe banana, frozen
1 cup unsweetened almond milk or water
1 cup blueberries, cantaloupe, or pineapple
2 tablespoons ground flaxseed
2 handfuls spinach

Place all ingredients in a blender and mix well.

Easy, Breezy Banana Pancakes

2 organic eggs, whisked
1 ripe banana, mashed
Raw honey
Berries (optional)
Chopped walnuts or pecans (optional)

Preheat a nonstick skillet on medium to low heat. Add a little olive oil, if needed, to keep eggs from sticking. Whisk the mashed banana into the eggs. Mix well. Pour about ⅓ of the mixture into the pan. Let cook for about 2 minutes before flipping. These are tricky to flip as they are very thin, almost like crepes. It may take some practice to get the hang of this. Flip and cook an additional 1–2 minutes. Makes about three pancakes. Serve warm with berries or nuts and warm honey.

Hampton's Chicken Salad

1 boneless, skinless chicken breast, roasted
1 avocado, chopped
3 green onions, chopped
2 tablespoons extra virgin olive oil
2 cups broccoli
2 cups grape tomatoes, halved
¼ cup mayonnaise (made with olive oil)
3 tablespoons spicy brown mustard
2 tablespoons stoneground mustard
Himalayan salt, to taste
Black pepper, to taste

Preheat oven to 375 degrees. Season chicken breast with salt and pepper. In an ovenproof skillet, heat olive oil and sauté chicken breast. When chicken pulls away from pan, remove from heat, and turn breast over. Continue to cook in the oven for 7–10 minutes. In a medium saucepan, bring water to a boil and add broccoli. Cook approximately 5 minutes, then remove from heat and drain. Transfer broccoli to a bowl with ice water to slow down the cooking. In a large mixing bowl, add avocado, green onions, tomatoes, drained broccoli, and chopped chicken. Season with salt and pepper. Mix together the mayonnaise and mustards and add to salad.

Spinach, Tomato, and Onion Frittata

6 organic eggs, whisked
3 green onions, chopped
½ yellow squash, chopped
5 grape tomatoes, halved
1 cup spinach, chopped
¼ cup feta cheese, crumbled
2 tablespoons extra virgin olive oil
Avocado, chopped (optional)
Himalayan salt, to taste
Black pepper, to taste

Preheat oven to 375 degrees. In a large skillet, heat olive oil on medium heat and add green onions and yellow squash. Season and sauté until tender. Add spinach and tomatoes and toss with other vegetables. Transfer sautéed vegetables to a medium baking dish. Spread over the bottom. Salt and pepper whisked eggs and pour over vegetables. Sprinkle crumbled feta cheese over egg mixture. Cook approximately 10–15 minutes or until eggs are set. Cut and serve with avocado.

Avocado Toast with Poached or Scrambled Eggs

2 slices Ezekiel bread (found in freezer section of grocery store)
1 avocado, mashed
2–3 organic eggs, scrambled or poached
Himalayan salt, to taste
Black pepper, to taste

Toast 2 slices of Ezekiel bread and spread avocado on toast. Add a poached egg on each or divide scrambled eggs on top. To poach an egg, bring a skillet of water to a simmer. Crack eggs into water. Lower heat and continue to simmer for about 5 minutes. Turn off heat, cover with a lid and let cook an additional 3–5 minutes. If using poached eggs, drizzle a little olive oil on top, and add salt and pepper, to taste.

Spinach Fruit Salad with Roasted Chicken

1 boneless, skinless chicken breast
2 handfuls baby spinach
¼ cup blueberries
¼ cup strawberries, quartered
½ orange, peeled and cut in pieces
¼ cup dried cranberries
¼ cup walnuts, almonds, or pecans, chopped
½ lemon or orange
Extra virgin olive oil
Himalayan salt, to taste
Black pepper, to taste

Preheat oven to 375 degrees. In an ovenproof skillet, heat 2 tablespoons of olive oil, and sauté seasoned chicken breast. When chicken pulls away from pan, flip and finish in the oven for 7–10 minutes. Combine the next seven ingredients in a large bowl. Slice or cut up chicken into small pieces and add to salad. Squeeze a lemon or an orange and add a splash of olive oil. Salt and pepper, to taste.

CHAPTER 7

Move to Live

One Day at a Time to a Lifetime

"Take care of your body…. It's the only place you have to live."—Jim Rohn

W e humans are in a very strange time in our evolutionary history. In the past 50 to 100 years, something incredible and unprecedented happened…we stopped moving. (Personally, I think it started with the wheel, or maybe it was that pesky industrial revolution and Mr. Ford's assembly line.) Whatever started it, we have ended up here, in 2015, where we have taken the need to move out of our living equation. It simply isn't necessary anymore.

Just a few hundred years ago, living on the earth meant moving on the earth. The primary mode of transportation was walking (or running). To most people, a job meant lifting something, carrying something, or building something heavy that needed to be lifted or carried.

There was a small group of those with wealth or power of some kind who were carted around and didn't have to work too hard, but everyone else had to do things—physical things. A few hundred years before now, those things were harder, and living meant walking farther and pulling, lifting, and pushing heavier things around. Go back far enough and you'll find a static period in our evolution where the human body was in almost constant motion. Moving was an essential part of staying alive. If our ancestors sat still for half as long as we do in a given day, they would quite simply be dead. The human body was designed to move.

Today, technology has taken movement out of our lives. We no longer have to get up to answer the phone or change the channel on the TV. Even shopping has been somewhat relegated to the push of a button. All of these things can be done within an arm's reach on our cell phone, iPad, computer, or remote control. We don't even have to leave the comforts of our sofa. Not only has this technology made our lives as adults sedentary, but it is affecting our kids as well. Just 20 years ago, kids were playing outside, riding bikes, and participating in neighborhood sports; moving was part of life every day, all day. That's not so anymore. We are raising a generation of kids who are inactive, overweight, and unhealthy.

"So what?" you might say. Well, the problem is that we haven't designed our bodies out of our lives. We still have them, and they **ARE** designed to move. It seems all we're using them for is a good place to hang our clothes. For the most part, we use them like Sir Ken Robinson joked, as a "way to get their heads to meetings." With the exception of the common pet, no other living creature uses its body less than we use ours. Our bodies are the only mechanisms that get better when we use them, and worse when we don't.

A body that moves often feels better, works better, thinks better, looks better, gets sick less often, and is less likely to get an injury. A body in motion experiences the world in a totally different way, too. Sleep is more restful and rejuvenating, thoughts are clearer and more focused, and sex is better for a body that moves and moves often.

Walking Is the Superfood of Fitness

Walking is a great way to improve and maintain your health. It takes only 30 minutes a day to improve cardiovascular fitness, reduce excess body fat, strengthen bones, and increase endurance. It is something you can do every day and anywhere. It's free and doesn't require special equipment or training. This is a low-impact activity that most anyone can add to his or her daily routine. It can be done alone, incorporating meditation as part of the exercise, or with a group of friends to make it a fun, social experience.

Scientist Katy Bowman says, "Walking is a superfood. It is the defining movement of a human. It's a lot easier to get movement than it is to get exercise." She goes on to say that it is as important biologically as eating. Walking is the most natural movement we make. Unless you have a disability, you can walk. It is probably the easiest way to begin putting movement back into our lives.

Posture is very important when walking. You should keep your head up and looking forward, not at the ground. Your neck, shoulders, and back should be relaxed, not stiff. Swinging your arms is a good way to bring upper-body movement into your walk. Slowly increase your walk to a brisk pace. As your fitness improves, add more intensity to your routine by walking up hills, increasing speed and distance, and walking longer.

Sitting Is Killing Us

That may sound drastic, but some are saying, **"Sitting is the new smoking**." Research has shown that sitting for long periods of time is linked to obesity, increased blood pressure, high blood sugar, cardiovascular disease, and even cancer. According to Dr. Eric Tepper, sitting for hours is tied to all of these chronic diseases, regardless of age. Some doctors are even calling it the "sitting disease." If you think about it, we are sitting for most of our day. We sit at meals, we sit driving to and from work, we sit at work, and we sit to watch TV in our leisure time. That's a lot of sitting! I don't see much room in there for real moving unless, maybe you make a conscious effort to do so—for example, going to the gym, walking your neighborhood, or making lifestyle changes at the office or even at home. Even an hour or so at the gym after work isn't enough to negate the health risks of all that sitting. Experts are saying we should get up every hour and move for at least ten minutes. There are things we can purposefully do to incorporate more movement into our daily lives.

- Take the stairs instead of the elevator, escalator, or moving walkway.
- Walk for 30 minutes on your lunch break.
- Stand while talking on the phone or eating lunch.
- Replace your traditional office desk with a treadmill desk or standing desk (new trendsetting idea).

Dr. Tepper says, "The people who really have that lifelong activity, they're doing great when they're in their 90's."

We have to design movement back into our lives, and we have to do it in a way that recognizes and appreciates the world we have designed for ourselves. The impact of movement—even leisurely movement—can be profound. We can't all quit our day jobs and chop wood for a living, but we can make daily changes that will make a difference in the health of these bodies we have been given. We can design some time every day to move in a way that respects our bodies' need to move, while at the same time, meeting our need to get on with our lives, our families, our work, our interests. Getting up every hour and moving ten minutes is a way to get our bodies moving again and turn everything around. Just as we must feed our bodies on purpose, we must move our bodies on purpose.

Full Advantage Workout
We can't move all day, but we can move in such a way that when we exercise, we take full advantage of the time we have and the

movements we make. One way to do that is with my Full Advantage Workout. The Full Advantage Workout is a method for training and exercising I've developed that I believe is the most sustainable exercise methodology to create an ageless body.

The Full Advantage Workout is a way of moving your body through an exercise routine that takes full advantage of each minute and each motion made.

If you're going to exercise—and you are—use that time as efficiently as possible. There can be a huge difference between showing up to a workout and actually doing something of value while working out. Health clubs and gyms are full of people whose intentions are good, but few gym goers achieve results. While I respect the fact that they show up at all, and any motion is better than no motion, I see so many people who spend hours in the gym getting minutes of results. I want you to spend minutes in the gym (or your home) getting hours of results.

Motivation gets you started; **habit** keeps you going. I am not talking about anything easy. Like reaching any worthwhile goal, creating an ageless body won't be easy, but it can be a lot easier than you think if you persistently

- show up to your workouts
- take full advantage of the time you work out
- take full advantage of your movements when you work out

Showing Up

You should treat your appointment with the gym or your home or wherever you choose to exercise as the most important and unbreakable meeting of the day. It is actually very important. Your health is what makes everything else in your life possible. Being faithful to your fitness goals is being faithful to everything and everyone else in your life. Making the time to exercise is putting the oxygen mask on yourself before helping others around you, as we say in the airline business. It is simply irresponsible to treat other things as more important than your health and fitness.

Imagine if you canceled other things the way some people cancel their workouts when they feel other things are more important. You don't hear people say, "You know, I couldn't shower this week. I've just been so busy," or "Brush my teeth? Who has time for that?" If you are serious about changing your habits and living a healthful, vibrant life now—and I think you are if you have read this far—you must show up to your own workout and do the work.

Full Advantage of Time

Between the ages of 46 and 52, I won or placed in nine bodybuilding and fitness competitions. From February 2010 to February 2011, at the age of 53, I climbed four of the Seven Summits. A year ago I summited the fifth mountain, Mount McKinley in Alaska. I have never spent "hours a day" working out or training. My day in the gym consists of a 10 minute warm-up on an elliptical machine, 20 minutes of stretching, and 45 minutes of strength training.

Take a look around the gym. Time is being wasted in a lot ways. People stand around "talking" and socializing or are preoccupied with their phones. Other people seem to move through their routines with little purpose or effort, or they work through the exercise incorrectly. When you are at the gym, you should be doing something to achieve your fitness goals every minute you are there. After all, your time is very valuable.

My workout routine consists of one exercise followed by another and another until the time is gone. I am fully focused on my goals and achieving them. Done properly, a workout routine can be a fully aerobic workout as well. You should go from warm-up and stretching, then on to your exercises—not rushing or moving fast, but purposefully moving through the routine.

Stretching to Stretch Your Life

A warm-up must be a part of your exercise regimen. This would consist of exercises performed immediately before your main activity to increase your circulation and your heart rate. A big misconception is that stretching is warming up. In fact, static stretching does nothing to increase core temperatures and circulation. Any good trainer will tell you that a general warm-up should precede a stretching routine. What is a warm-up? It can be anything from light calisthenics, jogging, and jumping rope, to a recumbent bike, elliptical machine, or treadmill. Your warm-up session should last for a minimum of 10 minutes with a goal to increase blood flow and raise core temperature.

Static stretching is stretching to the farthest point and holding that stretch. Standing straight and bending over to touch your palms to the floor is a good example of a static stretch, which 9 out of 10 people cannot perform. This stretching is very similar to Hatha Yoga, which has been around since the 15th Century. Static stretching is by far the safest of stretching methods. If you are serious about your health and taking full advantage of your workouts (and I'm sure you are), spending 20 to 30 minutes a day stretching may be the most important part of your regimen. Along with the increased flexibility in your ageless lifestyle, it will also decrease injury during workouts.

Benefits of a warm-up:

- Increase blood flow
- Increase core temperature
- Increase heart rate
- Increase muscle efficiency
- Great preparation for the individual psychologically

Advantages of static stretching:

- Simplicity
- Easy execution
- Induces muscular relaxation

Guidelines for warm-up and stretch:

- Warm-up before stretch
- Have a positive attitude
- Breathe at a normal rate
- Develop a smooth tempo
- Use proper posture and form
- Move slowly into the stretch
- Do not force a stretch
- Let gravity pull you into a stretch
- Hold the stretch between 10 and 30 seconds
- Concentrate and focus

Being More Flexible

When it comes to physical fitness with the every day at-home athlete, stretching and flexibility are a total unknown or all but forgotten. Whether you are a stay-at-home mom or busy executive, your body is your instrument, and proper stretching must be incorporated into your routine if you want to live an ageless lifestyle. By being more flexible, you can reduce the rate at which you age, and flexibility can be developed at any age.

Full Advantage of the Motion

Not only is time wasted in the gym, but motion is also wasted. We have all noticed the "grunters" in the gym. Usually clad in tank tops or tight-fitting tees, they load up plate after plate of weight and push or pull it through a range of motion in one direction, relax, and let gravity do its thing, then repeat. They swing their bodies to create inertia or lean back and arch to create some angle to make the curl easier or the too-heavy squat possible. They are cheating, and the only ones they are hurting are themselves.

Injuries aside, at least they are in the gym (which is better than being on the couch), but they waste a lot of effort and motion by failing to pay close attention to three truths. When moving through your routines, understand and believe the following:

- **Form Matters More than Anything:** The difference between doing an exercise and doing it with perfect form is huge. Form, when working out, isn't just important; form is foundational. If you get the form wrong, then everything else you do—weights, reps, resistance, etc.. --- is simply more of the wrong thing. The price to pay for improper form is injury and, of course, a less effective use of your time and effort.

- **The amount of weight lifted matters less than anything:** Perhaps the silliest and most meaningless question ever used to gauge a person's fitness is "How much can you bench?" Unless it is your goal to win a bench press contest, the numbers on the weights are meaningless. Four years ago I won the Musclemania Mr. Natural Universe competition. How much weight did I train with? I can't tell you. I simply don't remember. What I can tell you is that I used the right amount of weight to keep proper form throughout the exercise. That was a lot lighter than you might think. The number on the weights, like your age, is meaningless.

- **Use everything you have every time.** When you exercise your biceps, your legs should be working. When doing leg presses, your shoulders and arms should be flexing. Your abdominals and core muscles should always be flexed and tight. It requires total focus of your attention on every muscle you have. (If you are wondering where the hard part was, this is it.) With every exercise you do, fully activate every muscle you have. Remember, you should make maximum use of every motion during your workout. You should lower the weight with the same focused intensity that you used to raise the weight. Turn each exercise into a full-body experience that uses every inch of every movement to work the muscles in motion and even the ones that aren't moving. This is the fundamental difference between the workout I do and the workout done by most. By engaging your entire body in every movement, you can maximize the effectiveness of your workouts—using very little weight and minimizing the risk of injury that can take you off your routine. In fact, in all my years of training, I have never been injured during a workout.

This kind of focused and full-body engagement will take time to perfect. Instead of just pushing the weights through space, you are going to find yourself intensely concentrating on every move you make. Your pace may be very slow at first as your body gets used to the idea of flexing your forearms to exercise your legs or tightening your abs to work your shoulders. If you have never flexed the muscles in your body, it can be an intense experience. (Tip: Remember to breathe. Most beginners hold their breath during an exercise.) With experience and consistency, your motions will feel more natural, and you will find a rhythm to your training. With proper form, the right (small) weights, and using your whole body, you can dramatically change your life and how you look.

Now What?

You may have noticed that I just told you how to do something without telling you what exactly to do. That's because I don't know exactly what to tell you to do. I would have to know what your goals are, what your body type is, what body weight you would like to be, and how you want to look. Maybe you don't need to lose any weight at all. You may be comfortable and committed to your current exercise program.

Different goals affect the way you should start an exercise program. What I will tell you is to be cautious of canned programs that are good "for everybody." My personal goal for the moment is to prepare a plan for training to climb Mount Vinson Massif in Antarctica at the end of 2015 and Mount Everest in March 2017, and somewhere in between to ski to the North and South Poles. I wouldn't recommend my workout as a wellness maintenance program for everyone. So, for now, just do an honest assessment of where you are and what your goal is. If you did the goal setting in Chapter 1, you have already done that assessment. If not, here's another chance. Take a good look at yourself in the mirror and answer these questions: what do you like about your body, what would you like to change, when would you like to make those changes, and why?

DR. ROXANNE CARFORA ON EXERCISE

"Age has no limitation to movement…. We may be slower, but we're still in motion."

As Tom has said, "You do not have to go to a gym and spend hours there. You just have to keep moving." Whether we are sitting in a chair, lying in bed, walking with a cane, or even sitting in a wheelchair, we are able to move our bodies. I had a 75-year-old patient who came in to see me recently and who got down on the floor and did ten push-ups. Another patient showed me how she "danced with her walker," and another demonstrated how she exercised in her wheelchair by lifting her arms up and down. These are just a few examples of how there was no gym, no hours, and no equipment (except the walker) involved. They had their bodies and used them. Personally, I incorporate **bursts of exercise** during the course of my day. It may be going up and down the stairs in between seeing patients. By the end of the day, I have gone up and down those stairs 20 times. My staff and I do lunges in the hallway of the office, push-ups at the counter, and squats in the lunchroom, and we pretend to do fast boxing (quick jabs) when we see one another in the hallways. All of these "small bursts of energy" supply us with boosts of adrenaline throughout the day. It takes just one person to start this in the office, and you will see how much fun you can have. Think of ways you can move more during your day.

CHAPTER 8

Health Is Your Wealth

Wealth Is Meaningless Without Health

"Man sacrifices his health in order to make money, then he sacrifices money to recuperate his health."—Dalai Lama

D uring my travels around the globe, I have had the opportunity to work with some of the super rich. I am positioned in one of the wealthiest demographics in the world, New York City and the Hamptons of Long Island, and I continually observe the pursuit of financial wealth with a total disregard for one's physical well-being. Some of the wealthiest individuals I have had the privilege to fly are among the most unhealthy. Building that business or climbing that corporate ladder of success seems to trump everything else in their lives; it's the highest priority, what seems to matter most. I am here to tell you this is wrong thinking. It's backward! Our success pyramid is upside down. Good health and energy are essential to success. You pay the price of bad health. You enjoy the price of good health.

The parallels between financial health and physical health are significant. Stress from one affects the other. Here are some ways in which there are similarities between the two:

- First step: Recognize there is a problem. More times than not, we wait until there is a crisis before we choose to change our lifestyle, whether it is a lifestyle of spending or a lifestyle of poor nutritional choices.
- There is no quick fix: 30 days, 60 days, or 90 days... Disease did not happen overnight, therefore the solution will not happen overnight. The state of our finances didn't suddenly dry up; the decline happened over time. There is no magic pill or lottery ticket.
- It is a lifetime commitment, a way of life. Our health and our finances require a permanent solution, not a temporary one. You must make a lifestyle change.
- Education is a key part of the process. Knowledge is the key to understanding what our bodies need and what our bottom line has to be.
- Accountability with others is vital to success. It keeps us focused on the goal at hand. Being accountable to someone or something keeps us from regressing to old habits.
- Philosophy matters in how you respond to a problem. Your belief system gives you the focus to stay committed to confronting and changing the problem.
- Great financial or health foundation is key to building a great family or a great business. You cannot build a family or a business if you are physically sick. You cannot build a family or a business if you are financially sick.
- Treat each in a holistic way: whole finances, whole body. When one part of our body is sick, it affects the whole body. When we feed our body, we feed the whole body. When our finances don't add up, it's not just the mortgage that is affected, but all aspects of the budget.
- Change preconceived ideas of how you look at finances and health.

- Sacrifices are part of successes in both finances and health. It's not always what you put in, but what you leave out. If you don't bring home the foods you don't want to eat, they won't be there to tempt you. If you want to save some extra money every week, you will sacrifice the daily Starbucks and make coffee at home. Sacrifice what you don't want in your life.
- Success has to be process driven, not product driven. Process is more important than product. There is no vitamin or supplement that will take the place of eating whole foods with the purpose of nourishing our bodies. Financial success cannot happen without managing our money and investments to our advantage.
- Because we are living longer, we need to be financially and physically healthy. Investing in your health today is key to preventing illness tomorrow. Sound planning and investing today is necessary for the security of tomorrow.
- Financial and physical health do not fit into one mold; each is individualized to our own needs. When I am preparing for my next climb, my fitness needs will be different than yours. My financial needs won't be the same as someone else's.
- Income is key to finances just as nutrition is key to health: each is essential to its corresponding foundation.

———

DR. ROXANNE CARFORA ON TREATING LIFE AS A GIFT

"Our bodies deserve the respect of acknowledging how hard it was to be created."

Our chances of being born are about 1 in 30 million. That, in itself, is a miracle! We all know life is priceless, but we don't treat our bodies as the precious gifts they are. Each of us has a purpose on this earth and a responsibility to ourselves, as well as those we bring into our lives—family, friends, partners, employers, employees, and anyone else who depends on us. The choices we make every day regarding health and finances will impact our future and the future of our families. They both determine the quality of life we lead. **With better awareness, we make better choices; with better choices, we get better results.** We do not have control over the costs of health care or insurance premiums, but we do have control over whether we spend our money to be sick or to be well.

———

Our health has to be more of a priority than our stock portfolio. How can we take care of our family or take care of a business or build a career if we can't get out of bed in the morning? We've all heard flight attendants give a briefing before a flight. One of the instructions they give is to put the oxygen mask on yourself first and then on your child. If you are not there to help, what good are you in case something unforeseen happens?

You aren't wealthy until you have something money can't buy. Unfortunately Steve Jobs knew this all too well. When a crisis occurs in our lives, whether it is financial or health, we wish we could go back and change the cause of the crisis. In hindsight, when we lose our health, many times it's too late and other times it is not. If we knew for certain that our decisions could change the outcome, we would do what we needed to do to fix it. Steve Jobs had many ups and downs financially, but he always found a way to overcome the adversities. I believe that if his health had been as important as his success, he could have won that battle, too. I'm not necessarily saying it's that simple, but I am saying that what we can do to change our health is more simple than we believe. My point is that all the money and technology in the world can't always save us. It's up to the choices we make regarding what we chose to nourish and heal our bodies naturally.

CONCLUSION

I don't know about you, but I am planning to live to 120, and I am planning to live well! This book is my message about how to live an adventurous, passionate, ageless life. I am not just giving you information. I am living these words. I am certain that if I can do it, you can do it, too. It doesn't matter when you start (it's never too late), where you start, or how you start, but that you take the first step to live the extraordinary life you have been given.

"The one thing you have that nobody else has is you…your voice, your mind, your story, your vision. So write and draw and build and play and dance and live only as you can."—Anonymous

———

ACKNOWLEDGMENTS

I would like to express my gratitude to everyone who has believed in me and encouraged me along this path that I have chosen…a path to live my dream life and change lives for the better along the way. I have my dark days, for sure, but as a wise sage once said, "Every passing moment is another chance to turn it all around."

I am infinitely grateful to Rhonda Kitchen, my partner, my best friend, and my angel who has supported me, pushed me, struggled with me, and loved me through the writing of this book. To my son, Brandon, thank you for your influence on my life, for your enthusiasm of my dreams and adventures, and for making me proud to be your father. I wish to thank Dr. Roxanne Carfora, who collaborated with me on this book and gave validity to the ageless lifestyle we are all looking for. Her input was invaluable to the ideas and philosophy I have put forth. To Mark Kutch, thank you for your encouragement, your vision for my message, and your contribution to the prescription scripts in each chapter. A special thank-you goes to Maria Dismondy, award-winning children's book author, for coaching me through this process and showing me the steps to take this book to the highest level.

Finally I want to thank those who have climbed the highest peaks around the world with me. I have met some incredible people who have made me a better, stronger, and more grateful person.

I especially want to recognize Geoff Schellens, one of my guides on Mount Aconcagua and Mount McKinley. His encouragement, patience, and expertise helped me realize some big dreams, and for that I am grateful.

———

ABOUT THE AUTHORS

TOM FABBRI is a world-class adventure athlete, dual-rated jet and helicopter pilot, author, chef, personal trainer, mentor, award-winning Natural Mr. Universe (age 50), and all-around life wrangler. Tom has learned to harness his fears while achieving his dreams and living a life on the edge. Whether he is climbing the highest peaks around the world, chasing the sun at 45,000 feet, or diving with great whites, he pursues life with passion. His journey to get here was paved with adversity, however. After hitting rock bottom many times, Tom found a vision and purpose that changed the direction of his life. He wants to show others how they, too, can live their dreams. His philosophy begins with a plan of optimal health and fitness that is pure and whole. Tom believes we can all attain an ageless lifestyle filled with adventure, fun, and passion.

DR. ROXANNE CARFORA is Board Certified in Anti-aging and Functional Medicine and trained as an Osteopathic Physician. She has completed a fellowship in family medicine. The combined philosophy of these specialties is to determine the "cause" of disease and correct the underlying nutritional and hormonal deficiencies *naturally* so patients can achieve *lifelong health and wellness.* Dr. Carfora has been practicing medicine on Long Island (where she lives with her husband and two beautiful children) for more than 20 years. She is an associate professor at New York College of Osteopathic Medicine and trains many healthcare professionals in nutritional medicine. She is an international lecturer on women's healthcare and hormonal imbalance. Dr. Carfora has published healthy living articles in *Image* magazine and *Newsday*, as well as appeared on local radio and TV. Her passion is to *educate, empower, and encourage* all to achieve optimal health for a *youthful* lifestyle.

Tom and Dr. Carfora have a vision to educate anyone who wants to change the notion that life with disease is inevitable. They have a desire to show others the possibility of achieving great health through simple and easy steps that are sustainable. Together they will be spreading their philosophy and message through a company they created called unoVous, whose motto is "One You…Live It Well." For more information on podcasts, webinars, speaking events, and products, please visit unovous.com. Follow Tom's adventures at tomfabbri.com, and follow Dr. Carfora at drcarfora.com.

————